The PURPLE ONION

Reflections on Moments of Divine Intervention

PHIL GUARRASI

ISBN 979-8-88540-505-8 (paperback)
ISBN 979-8-88540-506-5 (digital)

Christian Faith Publishing
832 Park Avenue
Meadville, PA 16335
www.christianfaithpublishing.com

Printed in the United States of America

Introduction

This is a story about special moments in time and how they determine a person's life and legacy. I'm certain that every person can relate to particular, individual moments that affected their lives in either positive or negative ways. I know that many circumstances can be attributed to the choices we make or a person's DNA. But now that I have reached my eighth decade of life, I look back upon a number of specific and very well-defined moments that guided my life, and which I can only explain as divine intervention.

From our very origins and even at the moment of our conception, there are factors in place that determine so many things about ourselves. Whether we were born male or female, the color of our eyes and skin, our physical proportions, facial features, and our mental and intellectual capabilities are already genetically determined. At that point, from our very first breath, all of our human interactions begin to shape us. From these early years and beyond, the love, the nurturing, and the values that we were taught or not taught, begin to affect our thoughts and inclinations and finally our actions.

However, beyond all of these factors, there are individual events, or as a friend of mine calls *punctuating moments*, that can have a tremendous impact on how our lives evolve. This thought brings to mind one of my favorite poems, "The Road Not Taken" by Robert Frost, in which he tells of coming upon two diverging paths in a "yellow wood," and how they both hold promise and yet make "all the difference" in the end.

This book tells the story about some of these moments that really did make all the difference.

Chapter 1

MY FAMILY

I was born into a large Italian family, and the first six months of my life were rather unique. My father met my mother at a neighborhood dance hall in south Brooklyn during the Big Band Era in the early 1940s, but within a year, he was drafted into the army to fight in World War II. His most notable event during the war was taking part in the D-Day landing at Omaha Beach. He often spoke of the events that he witnessed during that day and took pride in what was accomplished. He spoke of soldiers being killed as soon as they hit the beach, and he helped a few wounded soldiers to safety, and understandably, he was looked upon as a hero in our family.

Once the war was over, he and many other Americans were awarded the Croix de Guerre by the French government, and he was always proud of receiving this honor and being part of this momentous event. He related many of his war stories throughout the years while sitting around the dinner table and also wrote his own memoirs a few years later relating to his experiences at the request of a British war correspondent.

My wife and I visited Normandy in 2009 and went to Omaha Beach. My father had passed away twelve years earlier. It was very surreal and emotional looking out over that beach where the Allies landed. The cemetery located just off this beach is still so perfectly maintained by the French government. The crosses of the over nine thousand soldiers who died in that invasion so many years ago were aligned in perfect symmetry. There was also a large circular monument there listing the names of all of these brave men who perished there in alphabetical order. As I looked over the names to where my father's name could easily have been, I felt a lump in my throat and had tears in my eyes as I realized that my existence was due solely to the fact that he survived that fateful day.

Once World War II was over, he and my mother were married a year or so after he returned home. I can only imagine the feeling of seeing her again, along with family and friends, after returning from almost two and a half years of being away.

When I was born in September of 1948, my parents were living with my grandmother and my mother's three sisters in a very small apartment on Twenty-Seventh Street in Brooklyn. It was so small that I still can't believe my parents were willing to live there as newlyweds, and the bedroom where they and I slept in was perhaps seven feet wide by ten feet long. When I questioned this years later, I was told that apartments were hard to find after World War II, but I assumed that it was most likely due to financial reasons that they decided to live there.

In addition, one of my grandmother's sisters owned the house and lived downstairs with her family. Therefore, throughout the first six months of my life, I was surrounded by not only my parents but also a doting grandmother, four loving aunts, and a few cousins. I would assume that I received continual attention every waking moment, and as a result, I must have been a very content and happy baby. In fact, I had my handwriting analyzed by a woman who was an expert in the field when I was around forty years old. Her analysis noted that there was a major event in my life at six months old. I was surprised when I read that statement because that was the point when my parents moved into their own apartment on Fifty-Second Street. It must have been traumatic to me to now be living with just my parents and most likely missing all of the other persons and additional attention that I had known every day since my birth. I am still amazed that this woman could somehow see this in my handwriting over forty years later!

So as I began to grow and become a part of my very large Italian family, I remember that we were always spending time with aunts, uncles, cousins, and grandparents. My mother and her sisters had many cousins because my grandmother also had four sisters, and the overwhelming majority of her cousins were girls. On my father's side of the family, he was one of six brothers and three sisters who were all married with children, and they also had many cousins with families who all lived in the same section of south Brooklyn. Looking at old family photos, it is astounding to see how many people were at our house on my birthdays and other occasions, and I always looked happy, which was only natural growing up with so many loving relatives at my side. As I look back on this early part of my life, I feel extremely blessed to have experienced this tremendous amount of love and support, and which has remained with me throughout my lifetime.

My first birthday party!
The women greatly outnumbered the men.

One of my earliest photos with Mom and Dad.

SOME ADDITIONAL FAMILY HISTORY

My father's parents were both born in Sicily and came to America as World War I was breaking out, and my mother's family originated from Naples, but both of her parents were born in America. My mother's maiden name was Spinelli, and her mother's family name was Polito. My father's mother had the infamous name of Lucretia Borgia. When I eventually learned the history of the name and that she was the daughter of Pope Alexander VI in the late fifteenth century, I wondered if it was possible that he was part of my lineage. That might not be anything to brag about since he was one of the most corrupt popes in history.

I don't recall hearing stories about my mother's ancestors or what it was like in Naples, but my father always knew that the Guarrasi family came from a town not that far from Palermo, Sicily, which he called Arcamo. In 2006, my brother, Rob, and his wife, Brinda, traveled with my wife and I on a Perillo tour of Italy, and the first three days were spent in Palermo. My brother Rob and I decided that if we had the time, we would try to find this village that the Guarrasis came from. I did locate the town which was named Alcamo, and which was a village lying a short distance from the seacoast about forty miles away from Palermo.

We had one free afternoon to spend as we wanted on the tour, and so we asked at the hotel if they could arrange for a driver who would take us to Alcamo that day. The concierge made the arrangements for us, and the next day, a man named Gabriel picked us up in a large Mercedes at the hotel around noon. He was a very nice gentleman in his forties, and we had a lively conversation about religion with him along the way. He had a large scar on his head, and he described how he had a terrible accident some years before and was given up for dead. He told us that while he was in a deep coma, Christ appeared to him and brought him back to consciousness. From that point on, he dedicated his life to Christ, and later became a minister at a Christian church in Palermo.

We mentioned to him that our son Tim also had a fractured skull when he was nineteen years old and that we were concerned about his healing and the path he was on. Gabriel took us to his church later that day where he led us in prayers for him. He then told us that Christ spoke to him and predicted that Tim would also eventually come to know Christ and that his life would change for the better. I believe that those prayers were answered because Tim is now forty-two years old and has a strong faith, a good job, a beautiful wife, and a beautiful baby girl.

When we arrived at Alcamo, we first stopped at the beach, which was a long, wide white sand beach, and it almost looked like we could be in Hawaii. There was a restaurant there, and after taking a number of photos, we decided to have lunch before going up to the village. Rob then gave his business card to Gabriel and asked him if there was a way to find out if any Guarrasis still lived in the town. When Gabriel saw our last name, he said that his best friend from college was Raphael Guarrasi, and he lived in Palermo. He called him as we were eating, and when we finished, he knew exactly where to take us.

As we drove through the streets and narrow lanes of this old village, I felt as though I was being transported back in time. All of the houses were old and made of stone, and most were attached to other homes. We finally arrived at a street corner and were amazed to see that the street sign said *Via Guarrasi*. Wow!

Gabriel then walked up to a house off the corner and rang the bell. A woman named Giuseppina answered, and he explained that we were Guarrasis on vacation from America. She welcomed us as if we were family and invited us inside. As it turned out, we were not related, but she had recently purchased the house and was totally renovating it. As she showed us around, we marveled at original frescoed ceilings and tiled floors, and it was a relatively large house. She knew that the Guarrasi family lived there some years ago but had no additional detail. We spent at least an hour there, and we exchanged contact information with her upon leaving.

We then walked to the next corner, which opened onto a small piazza, and there was a lovely stone church at one end. Since I heard from my father that many of the family in Italy were stonemasons, I wondered if they could have been involved with building this church a century or more ago. It was almost surreal walking around Alcamo for a few hours while trying to imagine what it was like for our ancestors there in the past.

We also learned that our family had been involved in wine making and that their label was named Tenuta Rapitala. As we read upon doing some research, a woman named Gigi Guarrasi, "a descendent of a great family from Palermo" as the article stated, "married a French count, Hugues Bernard de la Gatinais in 1968. Together they rebuilt the vineyards that had been destroyed by an earthquake, and resurrected this vintage with French influence. Their son Laurent still runs the winery to this day." Our day in Alcamo became one of the main and unexpected highlights of our trip and gave us a stronger sense of our family heritage, as there are still many distant relatives living in this area of Sicily. However, upon returning to our hotel, the concierge asked us about our day, and we replied that it was a wonderful experience. He was happy for us but mentioned that he had some concern about our driver because he was a substitute for the original driver, but no one seemed to know who he was or how he was contacted. His comments added to our mystique of how persons named Gabriel and Raphael played a part in this very memorable day.

Brothers and wives on the beach in Alcamo.

The Guarrasi home on Via Guarrasi in Alcamo.

Chapter 3

CLOSE ENCOUNTERS OF THE FIRST KIND: EARLY FRIENDSHIPS

At some point in our early years, we begin to understand our uniqueness, and all that we experience and learn is from the confines of our own individual being. We begin to interact with people outside of our family which continues to shape our identity. Unfortunately, we can never understand how it might feel to exist as another person or to experience their feelings, thoughts, or emotions. In that way, each person exists totally within themselves, living in their own personal universe as their life evolves. Fathers, mothers, sisters, brothers, wives, and husbands—those people are all so close to us, but it is still impossible to understand how it might feel to be one of them or see the world as they do.

I spent all of my childhood as well as all of my teenage years living on Fifty-Second Street, which was a typical, very noisy Brooklyn neighborhood of two- and three-family attached houses, and I grew up living in the same house with my cousin Don and his family. My parents waited some time before having another child, but my brother Rob finally arrived some six and a half years after I was born, and he began to receive the same love and attention that I experienced. An older Italian couple who were childless owned the house and lived on the first floor, but they didn't speak any English. The husband, Tommy Squadrito, passed away suddenly when I was twelve years old, and he was the first person that I knew who had died. His wife lived alone for the next few years but eventually moved back to Italy to live with family there. At that point, Don's parents purchased the house and moved into the first-floor apartment.

Don and I were separated by only six months in age, so we were best friends right from the start. When we turned five or six years old, we started playing with other children on our block. Our first friends were the three Durando brothers who lived only a few doors away, and they had four sisters. Soon after, we made friends with other boys and girls who lived close to us. In the 1950s, children played so many street games such as stickball, kings, hide-and-seek, and tag, and this kept us busy during long summer days. We were also good at just inventing new games to play. It was a very simple time, but a happy place to be.

As we grew older, we started to make other friends from school and from other streets. Most importantly, Don and I went to Saint Michael's Grammar School and were taught good Christian values which were strongly enforced by the Sisters of St. Joseph. After graduating from Saint Michael's in 1962 at the age of thirteen, I went on to Brooklyn Technical High School and began to evolve as a teenager and expand my horizons even further. My reason for choosing this school was mostly because I knew that my parents struggled financially, and I didn't want them to have to pay the tuition for a Catholic high school. So I traveled on the subway by myself every day to school and back and it was my first sense of independence and freedom, and it became one of the first roads that I had chosen on my own.

Don and I separated somewhat at that time in that he decided to go to St. Augustine High School. Throughout those years, we began to hang out with a wider group of friends, and we joined a neighborhood football team called the Bay Ridge Rams for which I played quarterback and wide receiver, and Don was the fullback. We started dating girls, and everything surrounding the Bay Ridge Rams became a big part of our social life.

By the time I turned sixteen years old, our crowd that hung out on the corner of Fifty-Second Street and Fourth Avenue was growing bigger all the time. Those years, however, seemed to pass too quickly, and soon my four years at Brooklyn Tech were over. It was then 1966, and I decided to continue my technical education and was accepted into the Polytechnic Institute of Brooklyn, or simply Brooklyn Poly as it was called. This was one of more highly regarded engineering colleges in the country at the time, and I was hoping to graduate with an engineering degree in the future.

The Bay Ridge Rams

Chapter 4

WHAT I REMEMBER
FROM THE 1960s

Since the majority of my teenage years took place in the 1960s, I believe that some comments are in order regarding that very turbulent decade and what we experienced. First of all, we lived under the constant threat of nuclear war with Russia, and this came to a head in October of 1962 with the Cuban Missile Crisis, in which war was narrowly averted. It was also the decade of the space race, race riots, the hippie culture, and the Vietnam War.

The Vietnam War fueled mass protests and talk of revolution as young men of eighteen were now being drafted into the army. Many persons escaped to Canada after being drafted to avoid having to serve in the military. Luckily, college students were exempt from the draft for the first few years, but they eventually instituted a draft lottery based on a person's birth date. I was again fortunate in that my lottery number was 246, and as a result, I avoided having to serve. Unfortunately, many of my close friends were not in college and were drafted. Hank, who lived just a few doors down the block from us, was wounded when he was hit by shrapnel and returned home as a result still nursing his injuries.

However, to most people, the assassination of President John Kennedy in November of 1963 was a moment that became permanently etched into everyone's memory. We were sent home early from school that day, and there was a stunning silence and tremendous sorrow everywhere. This lasted a number of days until his televised funeral a few days later. Martin Luther King Jr. and Bobby Kennedy were also assassinated within months of each other in 1968, and it was more of the same shock and horror.

So we experienced what seemed like constant turmoil, and this was aptly expressed in an article in the *New Yorker* magazine in statements which a Harvard professor and Nobel Prize winner named George Wald gave in a lecture in early 1969 titled, "A Generation in Search of a Future." In this talk, he noted that growing up with the constant threat of nuclear war had created an uneasiness and lack of hope for the current generation of young people. I can certainly agree that at times this seemed to be the case during those years.

However, the decade seemed to end on a more positive note when our country landed men on the moon in July of 1969, and we were able to watch those first steps taken by Neil Armstrong on TV. In addition, as a New Yorker, we watched and celebrated as Joe Namath and the New York Jets won the Super Bowl in January, and the Miracle Mets winning the World Series in October of that same year.

In spite of all of those momentous and troubling events, this was also an era of good times and especially great musical creativity with supergroups like The Beatles, The Rolling Stones, The Who, Led Zeppelin, The Doors, and so many more, as the doo-wop era of the '50s and early '60s was left behind forever. There was also Motown, The Four Seasons, and The Beach Boys. This great music seemed to help pull us though all of these terrible things that were happening. There was finally the Woodstock Music Festival in the summer of '69, and it was called The Summer of Love. Peace signs were being flashed everywhere, and The Beatles were mostly responsible for turning things around in people's minds. Somehow, everyone started to feel freer and less troubled.

But at the end of the decade, The Beatles broke up to everyone's dismay. Soon after, a new era of singer/songwriters emerged such as Bob Dylan, Elton John, Billy Joel, Stevie Wonder, Joni Mitchell, and Laura Nyro, which carried us into the 1970s.

The lyrics of Dan Fogelberg and Jackson Browne were always very meaningful to my brother Rob and I. Fogelberg sang in his song "Netherlands," "High on this mountain, the clouds are below, I'm feeling so strong and alive. From this rocky perch I continue to search for the wind, and the snow, and the sky." At that point in my life, I felt that I had reached some type of pinnacle and was also wondering and surveying what lay ahead. He goes on to sing, "I want a lover, and I want some friends, and I want to live in the sun, and I want to do all the things that I never have done." Well, I had many good friends but was looking for a lover and also wanting to experience many new things. Jackson's line in the song "Running on Empty" was also right on when he sang, "in 69 I was 21, and I called the road my own, I don't know how that road turned on to the one I'm on." Well, all of those lines just about summed it up for me. In '69, I was twenty-one, and I realized that I was very fortunate and blessed to have survived but also enjoyed the '60s, and I now had my dreams set on the future.

Chapter 5

DISASTERS AVOIDED

There were a number of incidents throughout those early years in which I escaped what could have been major life-altering events, and I would be negligent if I didn't mention a few of them. The one that comes to mind most readily is the one summer day when I was perhaps twelve years old. Don and I went to the Sunset Park swimming pool as we often did in summer. Just after changing in the locker room and putting on my bathing suit, I ran out and immediately dove into the three-foot pool without much thought and smashed my head into the bottom of the pool. I hit the bottom very hard but luckily only received a large bump on my forehead. It could have been so much worse. Many years later, an accident happened with a friend's son who was paralyzed from the neck down because of a similar mistake.

Another incident occurred one summer in my late teenage years when I was with a group of friends in Narrowsburg, New York. Narrowsburg was a very scenic town with a bridge that passes over the Delaware River connecting New York to Pennsylvania. There was a thick rope that was tied under that bridge, and young people were swinging out over the river while holding on to that rope and then being pulled back by another rope that was tied to it. A few people would also drop into the river and swim to shore. Both of these ropes were very thick, and the one that swung out over the river had a big knot tied to the end allowing a person to sit on the knot as they swung out.

When one of my friends sat on the end of the rope ready to take the ride, I was standing on the rope that was there to pull it back. So as he went out over the river, I was thrown to the ground by the power of the return rope that I was standing on by mistake. If that rope had wrapped around my leg, it would have pulled me off the cliff, and I do not believe that I would have survived. I was very fortunate to have God's protection in both of these situations.

One last incident that comes to mind involved my wife and me much later in life. As we were traveling in winter to go skiing in early 2003, we were driving in a snowstorm that was beginning to intensify as we were getting near the Vermont border. I got off the first exit from the highway to clean off the windshield and get more gas. We then got back on Interstate 91, but the snow continued to make it difficult to see, and soon we were driving in the deepening tracks of the previous vehicles on the road.

After about another ten miles of squeezing the steering wheel and trying to see the road, I needed to clean off the windshield once more. Therefore, I pulled off the highway again at exit 4, and there happened to be a hotel called the Putney Inn just across from the exit ramp. I once again cleaned off my windshield, and we went in to use their restroom. In about five minutes, we started again, and even though we were extremely apprehensive and concerned, we began to drive back toward route 91 north. We were still seventy miles away from our destination.

However, just as we turned onto the entrance ramp, we noticed a stalled truck that we could not get around. Therefore, our only choice was to take I-91 south for seven miles to the previous exit and then get back on to go north again. The idea of driving those extra fourteen miles made us realize that it was not a wise idea to try to complete our journey that night. Therefore, we backed off the ramp, went back into the Putney Inn, and were fortunate that they had an available room for the night.

It was quite amazing that the stalled truck was sitting right where it was. As we pondered that thought over a meal and a cocktail by a warm fire a short while later in their restaurant, the significance and magnitude of this event had us in awe. The fact that we would have most likely had an accident or possibly be stranded somewhere that evening had we been able to enter the highway again made us give thanks to God for this significant event.

IN SEARCH OF A CAREER

My college career, as I mentioned, began in September of 1966 at Brooklyn Poly, and I worked and studied hard over those four years with the hope of finding a good job upon graduation. I must admit that I found calculus and most engineering courses extremely difficult, and as a result, I added a few liberal arts courses to my last two years of curriculum. As a result, I graduated with twelve additional credits. However, these years were quite uneventful, and I still took the Fourth Avenue local each day to my college and returned home every evening, so I never had a typical college experience of living away from home. My original interest was in architectural engineering because I wanted to design homes, and I used to draw floor plans in high school.

However, in the midst of the space race in the mid-1960s, I decided to switch my major to aerospace engineering. With just a few months to go before my graduation, there were interviews at school with many of the major aerospace corporations. I applied to companies such as Grumman, Fairchild, and McDonald Douglas. Grumman was my preference because they were located in Bethpage, Long Island, and they had designed the lunar excursion module, which was the vehicle that landed on the moon in 1969. However, I never received an offer from any of these companies.

At that point, I was open to any offers or any opportunity that I might receive in order to have a job once I graduated. Going to graduate school was something that I never considered. I knew that I was totally done with sitting through boring engineering courses, and I knew that I was totally through with school. Many times, I questioned my choice and thought that I made a mistake for choosing an engineering curriculum in the first place.

However, one day in April of 1970, as I was walking through the hallways between classes, I came upon a notice posted on an index card at the dean's office saying, "Sales engineering trainee wanted, apply Dean Grau." This turned out to be one of those defining moments in my life that I later began to believe was divine intervention. I immediately knocked on the door and entered, and a secretary was sitting at the front desk. I explained that I was interested in applying for the job mentioned outside. She told me that she had just put that posting out just a few minutes before and that I should wait as she went to mention it to Dean Grau. The dean came out of his office a minute later and asked me my name. He said that I came in at a very opportune moment because he had the president of the company looking to hire this person in his office. He then invited me to come into his conference room to meet him.

Once inside, I was introduced to a Mr. Harold Kiernan who was a Polytech alumni, and they invited me to sit down at a very large luxurious oak table, and it resulted in a spontaneous interview. I don't remember feeling uncomfortable at any point in meeting the dean and Mr. Kiernan for the first time, and I thought that I handled all of their questions very well. I explained that I was never certain that I wanted to be an engineer, and the idea of becoming a salesperson would be of great interest to me since I believed that being a good communicator was one of my main assets. I must have made a good impression on both of them, and Mr. Kiernan invited me to visit his company in Lodi, New Jersey the following week to meet with his sales manager.

I had recently purchased my first car which was a 1969 Volkswagen Beetle, so I drove there the following week, and shortly thereafter, I was offered a position as sales trainee for Harold's company, which sold technical industrial products. So upon graduating in June 1970, with a bachelor of science in aerospace engineering and still just twenty-one years of age, I began working for Mr. Kiernan at his company Flo-Tek. Because of this, my career as a salesman began, and it enabled me to do what I know I was best suited for. It gave me a sense of freedom and led me to become a successful salesperson, which allowed me to evolve in so many other unexpected ways. I was able to form many rewarding relationships over the years and eventually started my own company, which has been very fulfilling and successful for the past thirty years.

Unfortunately, Flo-Tek experienced bad luck about a year after I began working there when their office and shop was flooded from heavy rains that hit New Jersey. As a result, Harold was forced to move to another location in Closter, New Jersey, but I continued to work for him for another few years, although the flood had hurt him financially. He and his wife attended my wedding in 1972, and their wedding present was a week at their house in Ocho Rios, Jamaica. That resulted in my wife and I taking the first plane trip of our lives, and it was a wonderful and amazing experience.

So whenever I think about how this all came about, I am still quite amazed. Had I not been in that exact place at that perfect time, this would never have happened. I sometimes wondered what type of job I might have found had I not seen the note that day. Most likely, I would have worked somewhere as an engineer, and I wonder if that would have been fulfilling to me. Oh well, this time I guess I could say that this event was just a matter of luck or coincidence. I guess that's one way of looking at it, but soon, other events happened in my life that made me think it was much more than that.

Chapter 7

THE QUEEN OF HEARTS

Just a few months later, it's the summer of 1970, and I'm getting comfortable in my new job and driving to Lodi, New Jersey every day. I was feeling really good about life as I made it through the turbulent era of the 1960s, and the Vietnam War was winding down. I guess things were almost getting back to a new normal. Don and I were still very close, and we had a very good close group of friends and were enjoying ourselves socially going out to bars and clubs, which seemed to be everywhere in the '60s and '70s. Everyone was into dancing, and as I mentioned, there was a lot of great music and performers that we enjoyed.

So on the Saturday night of July 11, 1970, I went out to a new club in my neighborhood called Carpenters Hall. It had been a union hall but had recently been converted into a dance club. My friends and I had just heard about it, so I went there with a friend on that beautiful summer night. I think we arrived before 10 o'clock, and once inside, I noticed a girl that had her back to me who was tall and shapely, with long blond hair. When she turned around, I saw that she was also very good-looking and so I decided to immediately go over and talk to her. I didn't hesitate since I was afraid that someone else would begin speaking to her first, and I would lose this opportunity. She was with a friend, so I said hello and introduced myself, and in a short while, I asked her if she would like to dance.

As we danced and talked, I knew that I was definitely interested and wanted to get to know her better. I was also hoping that she didn't have a boyfriend somewhere. In those days, as I'm sure it was in previous generations, every few songs were a slow dance, and it was easy to feel intimate with someone very quickly.

One very interesting thing about that night is that she went there with a girl named Valerie who she never went out with before, even though they lived on the same street in the Marine Park section of Brooklyn. She also had never gone to a club in this section of Brooklyn before, so how she wound up there that night and with Valerie was a mystery. As we danced, I asked her how they were planning to go home, and since she wasn't sure, I offered to drive them. We departed the club just after midnight, and I first dropped off Valerie, then drove her to her house. I was not familiar with this area of Brooklyn and was impressed by how nice the neighborhood was.

Before she got out, I asked her if she would like to go with me to Central Park the next day. She said yes, and so I picked her up that Sunday afternoon, and we had a nice time walking around the park on a very hot summer day. So we met on 7-11-70, her name was Barbara, and in less than two years, she would become my wife.

However, what makes this story even more amazing is what happened a few weeks after we were dating. My friends and I used to gamble at times, and we liked going to the racetrack and playing poker. One Saturday afternoon, not that long after I met Barbara, five of us were playing poker in my friend Walter's basement. One of the poker games that we usually played was called no peek. It was a game where all seven cards were dealt out to all the players face down. One by one, the players turned over cards until they beat the previous hand. The first two cards that I turned were the ten and king of hearts. The other players then continued to turn their cards until it was my turn again.

When I turned the next two cards and they were the jack and then the ace of hearts, I was quite happy in that I was very close to either a straight or a flush with three cards still to turn. I then turned my fifth card, and everyone was shocked when it turned out to be the queen of hearts. In just five cards turned, I had a royal flush in hearts.

Anyone who knows the game of poker would know how difficult this was, and what could possibly be the odds of this happening? I would guess maybe a few million to one.

Beyond that, what could be the odds of the queen of hearts being the final card that I would turn? It was absolutely unfathomable. I took this as an immediate sign that Barbara was the one, for what else could this possibly mean? I'm certain that any fortune-teller would've seen it that way. By the way, the actual odds of this happening are very close to thirteen million to one.

I often wondered if I had not met Barbara that evening who I might have married, what my children might have looked like, and where would I have lived. Everything in my life would have been very different. After renting an apartment for three years, our first home turned out to be right across the street from where she grew up on Marine Parkway, and we still live there to this day. However, just as God meant it to be, four years after we were married, we started our own family when Barbara gave birth to Eric. In another three years Tim came along, and five years later, Brian arrived on the fourth of July weighing twelve pounds three ounces. They were all days of God's miracles in our lives to remember and celebrate!

Barbara and me on our honeymoon in Jamaica.

THE SAGA OF WORTH GLENN

At this point, I'd like to digress briefly from the primary topic of this book and tell the story of my first trip to the racetrack in the summer of 1968. As I mentioned in the last chapter, my friends and I liked to play poker, but I can't recall how this began. However, I do recall frequent poker games taking place during most of my teenage years in our backyard during summers on Fifty-Second Street, and at times at different friends' houses. It was a good way to pass time during that era when we weren't busy playing sports. The stakes were usually just nickels and dimes, but in two or three years, we were up to quarter bets on every card, and as I mentioned in the last chapter, I once pulled an unimaginable royal flush in hearts.

As far as the racetrack was concerned, I used to hear my father talk about the horses a lot, and he occasionally went to the track with my Uncle Jim, whose actual name at birth was Vincent, and Don's father Willie, whose original name was Dominick. I was always puzzled why Italians often began calling someone in their family by some other name, never to be referred to by their original name again! Anyway, Willie was a great guy, but there were a couple of Willies in the family, and so he was referred to at times as Willie the Weep. When I asked my father how he got that nickname, he said it was because he always complained a lot when he lost while gambling.

Anyway, from time to time, I also heard my father tell my mother that he put bets in with a bookie named Johnny Clemente who always had a cigar in his mouth and looked as if he was worth a million bucks. He could usually be found at some point of any given evening on the corner of Fifty-Second Street and Fourth Avenue by the local candy store or bar. That corner was a special place where the fathers on the block could escape for an occasional hour after dinner, as they waited for delivery of the late edition of the *Daily News* or *New York Mirror*. My friends and I were also there many times at the same time, and it was an enjoyable place to just hang out, shoot the breeze, and people watch.

My father and Uncle Jim also had a good business friend named Otto Belladonna. I thought that Otto might have had connections to the mob because he was their very rich friend who was also always well dressed and ran a few different businesses in Brooklyn, but I could have been wrong because he was always a gentleman and a very nice guy whenever I met him. So one summer in the mid-1960s, I heard my father saying that Otto had just bought a bowling alley on Eighty-Sixth Street in Bensonhurst named Roll-A-Rama. Bowling was one of my favorite sports back then, and soon Dad was taking me with him on Friday nights to bowl with Otto, Uncle Jim, and the big boys. It felt good to be hanging out with my father and these older guys and I liked being there and it was part of my learning experience.

Another year or two passed, and I now hear Dad talking to my mother and telling her that Otto had bought a horse who was a trotter named Worth Glenn. At that point I had no idea what a trotter was, but I soon learned that trotters raced by pulling a cart behind them called a sulky, whereas the flats were races where jockeys sat on the horse's back. In New York, trotters ran at Yonkers and Roosevelt Raceways, and they had what they called drivers instead of jockeys. So one day after the horse had a few races, the word comes down from Uncle Jim that Otto was told by the horse's trainer that in the next race they would be going all out with Worth Glenn to get him to win. They would be getting the final word that he was ready the day before. Uncle Jim, Dad, and Willie were all prepared and ready to go to the Roosevelt Raceway that night hoping to make a killing.

Unfortunately, Worth Glenn came in seventh in an eight-horse race. Sadly, Dad had to hear it from Mom when he came home dejected, and I assumed that Willie the Weep wasn't much fun to be with on the drive back home. Otto made some type of excuse that the horse had bad racing luck and said the next race would be different. The next week they got word that this time the horse was definitely ready to win, but Dad decided to put a smaller bet on him with Clemente instead of going back out to the track. This time he improved to fourth place, but my father was angry and gave up on him.

However, with all this talk about Worth Glenn, I was suddenly interested and looked at the results in the newspaper the next time he ran in which he now came in third. So I spoke to Don and one of my other close friends John Costello. I pointed out that Worth Glenn was getting better every time he ran, and I suggested that we should go to the racetrack to bet on him on his next race. So looking at the newspaper that following Monday, I saw that he was in the second race the next night. I let Don and John know and told them that we all needed $10 each so that we could have an even $30 to bet. The plan was to put Worth Glenn in a two-dollar daily double with every horse in the first race, and put the rest on him to win, place, and show. None of us had much money to spend back then, and I usually walked around and went to school with no more than $5 in my pocket.

However, we all managed to come up with the $10 each to bet, along with a few extra dollars for admission, a program, and gas for my father's car that was then around 29¢ per gallon. He let me have his car from time to time, but I don't know what my excuse was that night for using his car. I didn't want to let him know what I was planning and that we were going to the racetrack since I was afraid that he then wouldn't let me take it. Just before leaving for the track that night, we happened to run into Hank's older brother Jim who was known as Jimbo. He got that nickname due to his enormous weight and we were always a little intimidated by him and so we tried to stay on his good side. We told him about where we were going, and he gave us $20 to put on Worth Glenn, $10 to win, and $10 to place.

Our adventure began a little after 6:00 p.m., and we wanted to make sure that we would get there on time. Roosevelt Raceway was in Westbury, Long Island, and we had never been there before, but we did arrive in their parking lot with plenty of time to spare. Racetracks were very crowded in those days before off-track betting or OTB as it was called came on the scene. I remember the feeling of walking through the gates and seeing the racetrack and the grandstand with the stadium lights already shining. So we looked at the program and made our way to the betting windows and put our bets in, then walked around and watched the horses warming up while waiting for the first race to start at 8:00 p.m. We didn't care who won the first race, but the horse that did win paid $17 to win. A few minutes later they posted the daily double payouts, and the payout if Worth Glenn won would be $302. Wow! With that amount plus our win, place, and show bets, we would be in seventh heaven.

We were all nervous as we watched the horses for the second race come onto the track. We could see Worth Glenn who was number 5, and his driver Joe Bonacorsa who was his driver in all of his previous races. We also looked at the odds board and he was going off at twenty to one and we keep doing the math and can't wait for the race to start. Finally, at about 8:25 p.m., the marshal calls the pacers, as they call it, and the horses line up behind a car with a gate as they start to come around the track. The car then pulls away and Worth Glenn makes a strong move toward the front of the race and takes the lead. Roosevelt has a half-mile track, so the horses need to go around twice to finish the one-mile race.

As they passed in front of us the first time, another horse had taken the lead so Worth Glenn was now second on the rail, and we were all hyperventilating as they went around the second time. What we didn't realize is that we thought we were standing at the finish line but were really at the sixteenth pole which was one-sixteenth of a mile from the finish. So as they came around the final turn, Worth Glenn was a few lengths back, but moved out and was catching up to the leader. We were all screaming as was the entire crowd as the horses were nearing the finish, but just as they went by us, we realized that he was in second place just a half-length back. Well, at least we would collect for place and show.

However, I was puzzled as the horses went by us because they were still going very fast with some being whipped by their drivers.

We still believed that he lost, but not a minute later, they posted number 5 as the winner at $41.20 to win, and we started jumping all over each other. We then realized where the finish line actually was. So we ran in to collect our winnings and all watched intently as the teller counted out $450 for us in addition to Jimbo's amount. We then ran at full speed out of the racetrack and to Dad's car where we locked the door and counted out $150 each. I think we laughed all the way home as we relived every single detail of every moment of that race. It also started a trend of the three of us starting to go to the racetrack almost every week for a while, and we quickly learned that winning was not always that easy.

Upon getting back to our neighborhood at only 9:30 p.m., we first went to Jimbo's apartment and told him the good news. His winnings were over $250, and for that night, we were his very best friends. We then went back to the corner wanting to boast about our winnings, and who is the first person we see in the candy store but my father. So in my state of euphoria, I asked him if he knew that Worth Glenn was running tonight. He didn't know, so I told him that we went to Roosevelt to bet on him. He asked me how he did, and when I told him that he won, he slammed his hand on the counter and cursed. He then asked me what he paid, and when I said $41.20, he slammed his hand and cursed again. He finally asked me how much I won, and when I told him $150, he said to make sure I gave $20 to my mother when I went home. I guess I should have kept my mouth shut!

And so ends a typical 1960s Brooklyn story, "The Saga of Worth Glenn."

THE BUSINESS MOMENT

Twenty years after beginning my sales career at Flo-Tek, I finally made the decision to start my own company. Picking a name was not too difficult since my high school was Brooklyn Tech and my college was Brooklyn Polytech. I decided that *tech* needed to be somewhere in my company name. Therefore, after giving it some thought, I decided on Technical Components Company. I did make a few moves after my initial three years at Flo-Tek and worked at Crown Controls, Honeywell, Components and Controls, and finally Mooney Brothers, where I was hired as sales manager.

When I started Technical Components, I worked the first three years out of my basement. I had formed many solid business relationships through the years and so I was able to find business with many of my existing customers, but especially Con Edison, which operated all of the power plants serving New York City. However, I was struggling to make a living and working hard for every single sale. My main product lines consisted of high-quality industrial valves and instrumentation products. After those first few years, I began renting a small office just around the corner from my home. I then hired my first employee, a part-time secretary, Linda Sheridan. The business tools of the day were a word processor, for typing out quotations; a fax machine, for sending documents; and a beeper, so I could be notified if anyone needed to contact me.

However, one day in early 1993, my breakthrough moment happened which changed the future for me and my company. On that memorable day, I was working in Manhattan and started driving on my way home. As I was heading toward the FDR Drive by going down Fourteenth Street, I was going to pass right by the Con Edison East River Power Plant which was one of my accounts. I knew that the day shift ended around 3:00 p.m., but it was just 2:15 p.m., so I decided that if I could find a convenient parking place near the entrance, I would make one more sales call. Sure enough, there was a spot to park very close to the front entrance, so I went into the plant where I knew most of the key people and wound up speaking to the instrumentation supervisor Fred Miura.

After a few minutes of conversation, Fred happened to ask me if I represented any companies that manufactured valve actuators, and he went on to explain that the company they had been buying them from had decided not to make actuators in the future for valve applications. I told him that I would look into it, and when I got back to my office, I began to search through the Thomas Register, which was a set of fifteen huge green books listing all types of products and manufacturers. It was the Internet of its day, and almost all major manufacturers were listed there. When I searched for electric actuators, I saw a number of big-name manufacturers, which I assumed were all being represented in the New York metropolitan region.

However, I saw the name Rotork which I was familiar with and decided to call their number. No one answered, but I was able to leave a message, and the next day, one of their regional managers called me back, and his name was Jim Halligan. We discussed this opportunity, and Jim asked me to meet him for lunch the next week at Gallagher's Steakhouse in New York. He would tell me years later that I would one day say that the best thing that ever happened to me in business was the day I met Jim Halligan. A truer statement was never made because his prediction came true. I set up a meeting at the East River Power Plant the following week, and Jim and I met most of the key people there. The result was that they decided to buy four Rotork actuators mounted to valves that I was already selling.

From that point onward, I had a good amount of success selling Rotork electric valve actuators to Con Edison and other accounts, and as a result, Jim made Technical Components the official rep for Rotork in the New York metropolitan area. Soon after, I was able to hire additional salesmen and expand into New Jersey. Whereas I once had to go out and find every sale that I made, I soon learned that Rotork had a following of its own, and with a brand-new technology just being incorporated into their products, it was a successful relationship from the very beginning.

From that day on my company grew, our sales grew, and we became specialists in the valve automation industry. In addition, my relationship with Rotork led to opening up new horizons and opportunities for traveling to many places I never would have gone because Rotork had sales conventions all around the world every other year. My first such trip that I was invited to was in 1995, in which Barbara and I traveled to Monte Carlo and in the following years, we went with them to England and Spain and these European trips led to me wanting to go back to Europe many times after that. They were all places and vacations that we will never forget, and we also made a number of lifelong friends during these trips who were all Rotork employees.

Who knows what would have become of Technical Components had I decided to pass by Con Edison without stopping that fateful afternoon or if there was no convenient parking place or if Fred Miura had not mentioned this to me? Everything would have surely been very different. It was another example of a moment in time that could have easily been missed but which had a tremendous impact on my life.

Chapter 10

SOMEHOW KILLINGTON HAPPENED

Skiing had always been a big part of my life, and I fell in love with the sport in my late teens when my friends and I went on a couple of weekend bus trips to Lake Placid, New York. I went skiing once or twice a year throughout the 1970s, and in 1982, Barbara and I bought a ski house just a few steps off the ski slopes at Camelback Mountain in Pennsylvania. From that point forward, skiing became our main family pastime, and Eric, Tim, and Brian all started to learn to ski at four years old.

We soon began expanding our horizons and started traveling to Vermont to ski at Okemo Mountain, which in the 1990s had become our favorite place to ski. We began renting homes there for many years, and some years we went to Okemo two or three times. We also planned occasional ski trips with other friends with young children and which all resulted in a lot of memorable vacations.

For quite a while, I dreamed of buying a ski house at Okemo, except for the fact that the prices were a bit out of our range for the type of house that I wanted. So after many years of skiing at Camelback and Okemo, I decided to book a one-bedroom lodging at Killington Mountain in March of 2002. Killington was only another fifteen miles further than Okemo, and Barbara, Tim, Brian, and I enjoyed our weekend there. It was in a community called Sunrise Mountain Village, which also had a very nice sports center.

The second morning that we were there, it was raining lightly, so instead of skiing, I decided to go to the community sports center. As I was sitting in the whirlpool with one other gentleman that morning, I began talking to him about the real estate in the community. I told him where I was staying, and he just happened to have an apartment that he owned in the same building, so I asked him if he knew of any that were for sale. He told me that there were a couple in his building that were selling in the $80,000 range. That sounded like a reasonable price to me and so I called that afternoon to set up an appointment with a local real estate agent to show us both apartments. I also asked the agent if she could show us some of the larger homes in the community.

The next day she showed us around, and we wound up looking at a four- and a five-bedroom home that were much nicer than anything I had seen at Okemo but at a lower price level. Barbara and I both loved the five-bedroom home that was located just a short walk from the ski slopes. We discussed this a short while and decided to make an offer the next day. After a week or two of negotiating, the seller and us agreed upon the price. It all happened so very quickly, and if it were not for being at the sports center that rainy morning and speaking to the gentleman in the Jacuzzi, this might not have happened. Once again, it was a moment that was destined to happen and which led to many enjoyable years of skiing at Killington and memorable times with family and friends.

Chapter 11

AND STILL OTHER SINGULAR MOMENTS REGARDING TIM

The way my son Tim found a job and a house were both due to a series of individual circumstances and moments that all tied together resulting in the ultimate outcomes.

Tim was in the midst of some difficult times in his life, and he had made some bad decisions along the way, but he was always resilient and intelligent. In 2012, he took a test for a job at the New York City Department of Environmental Protection to work at one of their sewerage treatment plants. He achieved a very high score and was put on a list to eventually be hired. However, years passed without hearing a word, but finally, in 2017, he received a letter saying that New York City was now starting to hire from this list. His initial interview in May was cancelled because he didn't arrive with the correct driving credentials, and six additional months passed with no further contact.

Around that time, my son Brian and I were at one of these New York City plants, and we were speaking to the plant manager, Eric Klee. Brian had been working at Technical Components for around seven years. We told Eric about Tim's situation, and he commented that he was sorry to have to tell us that New York City had stopped hiring from that list, and they were now hiring from what he referred to as *provisionals*, who were persons who had not taken any tests but were being hired due to personnel shortages at the plants. I was shocked and sad to hear that, and I informed Tim of the situation.

However, the next day, I decided to phone the DEP's personnel office and inquired for Tim. I spoke to a lady who was very helpful, and I had all of Tim's test details and information in front of me. I told her what happened at the initial interview and that I believe that he should still be considered for the job. She understood and said that she would look into this, and less than a week later, a letter arrived giving Tim a date to come for an interview. As a result, he was hired that December and began working at one of the plants in early 2018. That one moment with Eric Klee made all the difference.

About a year and a half later, Tim had started looking for a house to buy, and Barbara and I had gone with him to take a look at a few of them, but none seemed to be exactly what he was looking for. However, during the Thanksgiving weekend of 2019, there was a chain of events that led to him finding the perfect house. It happened to be the day after Thanksgiving. As I was sitting in the living room with my son Eric and his girlfriend Jessenia who spent Thanksgiving with us, I received a call from Anil Johari, who had been renting a house which I owned at Mountain View Village near Camelback for the past five years. Anil had called to tell me that his family would be leaving the townhome at the end of January because he had gotten a new job elsewhere. After I talked to him a while and wished him well, I mentioned to Eric and Jessenia that I would have to advertise the house to try to rent it again. Jessenia immediately mentioned that I should put a listing on Zillow, which was an Internet rental website that I had never heard of.

So the next day I began to explore Zillow, and I listed the house there, but at the same time, I began to look at homes for sale in the area of Tannersville, Pennsylvania. However, I also decided to look at homes in our own zip code in Brooklyn. The one house that jumped out at me happened to be only two miles away from us, so I decided to take a ride there the following Tuesday afternoon to just look at the outside. I parked close to the house and walked in front of it when suddenly, one of the ladies who lived there came out the front door. I decided to say hello, and I mentioned to her that I had seen her listing on Zillow and that my son was looking for a home. We began to talk for a while, and she told me that their family had just listed the house on Zillow two days ago. She told me some things about the house including improvements they had made, and she also gave me the name of the real estate agent that she used to list the house whose name was John Reinhardt. Therefore, I called John that very afternoon, and he let me know that he was just starting to show the house the next evening to two other persons. He said that if we wanted, we could see the house afterward.

When I spoke to Tim, he told me that he was going to work at 3:00 p.m. that Wednesday and so he wouldn't be able to go in the evening. I called John back and asked him if it was possible to see the house earlier in the afternoon instead, and he got back to me a few minutes later to say that he could show us the house around 1:00 p.m. Barbara and I went with Tim to see the house, and I immediately realized that this house had so many excellent features and required little or no maintenance. The asking price was also very reasonable for the condition that it was in. I spoke to Barbara and Tim briefly, then spoke to John outside, and since I was helping Tim with the down payment, I told John that we would be willing to pay the asking price for the house. I realized that if we had offered less, then the people who were coming later might have an advantage if they were to make an offer.

Two other coincidences that happened during our visit there were also noteworthy. Barbara just happened to know the uncle of one of the ladies who was selling the house because she saw him often as part of a church group who visited the elderly. While talking, they both realized that they had met each other previously at his one hundredth birthday party. It also happened that Barbara also knew John's cousin very well from our church. It just seemed like everything was falling into place as they accepted our offer the next day, and we began the process of helping Tim purchase this house which he moved into in April 2020.

The chain of events that led to this happening was nothing less than astounding. It was not just one singular moment but a succession of individual ones! For if my renter did not call to say he was leaving and if Eric's girlfriend was not there at that exact time, I would have never looked on Zillow, and we would have never known about this house. In addition, the timing of my drive by just as the woman came out of the house to give me the name of the real estate agent was also perfectly timed. Finally, all of the coincidences of knowing this lady's uncle and also John's cousin gave everyone a very good feeling about this arrangement.

As I mentioned earlier, more of Gabriel's prediction so many years ago in Sicily were coming to fruition in miraculous ways.

Chapter 12

A PURPLE ONION APPEARS

In previous chapters of this book, I've noted some of the major events in my life that originated from singular moments that could have easily been missed and which altered the path of my life. And although I've always thought of these moments from time to time, there was one minor event that happened one day that made me think more deeply about the fact that perhaps these happenings were not all just by chance, and maybe they should be seen as evidence of divine intervention.

Well, one day during the summer of 2019, I was shopping in a local supermarket for foods to cook at Sunday dinner, which I enjoy doing from time to time. As I made my way around the supermarket, I went first through the produce department and then the cheese counter and then through the rest of the store and finally to the checkout. I suddenly realized that I had forgotten to get one of the items that I was planning to use in my salad. This one item that my salads cannot do without happened to be a purple onion. I wanted to go back into the vegetable department to get just one of them, even though I thought there was a chance that we might have some at home, but I didn't want to lose my place in line to do this, so I decided not to.

However, as soon as I got to the front of the line, to my amazement there was one item sitting right there on the counter, and it happened to be a single purple onion. As I looked upon it, I was taken aback at how this possibly could've happened. For who would leave just one single purple onion at the checkout counter, especially just when I wanted one? I saw this as a sign of God trying to speak to me in a very strange way to get me to realize that just perhaps all of these moments that I've been wondering about in my life had not just happened by chance. Rather, it was by His design, and He had put all of those situations or circumstances or individual moments in my path all along the way because He had the ultimate plan for my life. He had been guiding my path throughout my entire life. It just took seventy-one years and a purple onion to make me finally realize!

Chapter 13

A ROAD NOT TAKEN

There are many situations over a lifetime in which opportunities become available, and decisions need to be made to either accept or reject them. I can recall a few of these circumstances during my travels in which a road not taken has made all the difference. There is no way of knowing the possible outcome of a decision not to take a certain path in life. Perhaps that path would have led to a much brighter place, or just maybe it could have turned out to be a road to nowhere.

One opportunity that was presented to me when I was in my midtwenties and which I chose not to accept comes to mind. At that time, Barbara and I were married just three years, and I was working for a company named Components and Controls. This company was located in New Jersey, and I was a salesman covering New York City and Long Island accounts. It was a relatively new company with a very ambitious president who had recently opened another location of the company in central Connecticut. His name was Lou Pettingill, and he asked me to meet him one day for lunch to discuss a new opportunity. His offer was for me to work for the new branch of the company to try to expand the business in southern Connecticut and Westchester County in New York. He offered to pay my moving expenses and give me a raise, and at the time, I was very open to doing this, so I told him that I would get back to him in a few weeks.

So Barbara and I discussed this possibility, and we decided to look for an apartment in the area of Tarrytown, New York which we did the next week. We looked at two apartments, and we liked the town and surrounding areas. However, after giving it a lot of thought and consideration, I decided to turn down the offer and remain as a salesperson for his company in New Jersey.

When I think back about passing on this opportunity, I don't recall exactly what my reasoning was. Perhaps it was because we were both reluctant to move fifty miles away from our families and also our close friends. So as a result, I remained at this company for a few more years before moving on to one more company prior to starting my own business in 1990.

There were many other situations during my life in which there were choices to be made and paths that were taken which made "all the difference" as Frost so aptly put it. It seems as though life is like a labyrinth, leading to a multitude of possible places and outcomes. Could there have been more happiness and fulfillment had I taken this diverging path so long ago, or would it have resulted in failure or regret? I also wonder if I had made the decision to accept this offer, how many other aspects of our lives would it have affected? The answer would have certainly been *every aspect*. Could Barbara and I have had different children, and how would they have evolved growing up in a different place? It's also very likely that I would have never started my own business, or if I did, it would definitely not have led me to an association with Rotork. Obviously, there's no way of knowing what could have been the final outcomes of this and all of the other roads not taken.

In Frost's poem, he seems to reflect upon one of the roads he had not taken at the end with regret. My only conclusion regarding all the paths that I have chosen is that I am happy, content, and thankful for the choices I made and for all of the divine moments that directed me. I can't think of many regrets, and I feel fulfilled for the life it has created for me and my family.

Chapter 14

THE SNOWBALL EFFECT

Sometimes there are events in your life that have a much greater effect on another person's life than your own. This situation has happened quite a number of times over my lifetime, and I thought it would be important to mention a few of them.

When I was in my early twenties, my friends and I went to Reber's Motel once or twice every summer. It was located in the scenic town of Barryville, New York, which was right on the Delaware River. Barbara and I had gone there when we were first married and then went many times afterward when our children were young, and we always went with Don, Kathy, and other close friends. So when my brother-in-law Ben Santoro mentioned that his father was looking to buy a piece of property, I immediately suggested that they come with us to Reber's one summer weekend. Before going, I put them in touch with Fred Reber who was also a real estate agent. A few weekends later, we rented a few rooms there, and Fred showed them land that was for sale. As a result, Ben's parents purchased a couple of wooded acres that they later built a house on and which continued as a family getaway until this very day. That one suggestion turned out to have a lifetime effect on the Santoro family.

There was also a time when I was out making sales calls in the mid-70s, and I noticed a company just across the avenue from my grammar school, Saint Michael's, named Industrial Instrumentation Services. I decided to stop in to see what this company did, and I met the owners Lee and Tony. As it turned out, they used the type of instrumentation products that I sold. In a short time, they began purchasing from me, and we quickly formed a good relationship. A few visits after I began doing business with them, Lee asked me if I had any friends that I could recommend because they were looking to hire someone to train as an instrumentation service technician. I immediately thought of my friend Frank who was unemployed at the time and said that I would ask him to give them a call. Frank did just that and was hired shortly thereafter.

He was employed by them for over ten years, but more importantly, as their company grew, he was able to get jobs for Don and three more of my other close friends at this company. However, after they all worked for Industrial Instrumentation for quite a number of years, Frank and John left and formed their own company. Then, just a few years later, Don also left and started his own company. All of their companies have been quite successful to this very day. So once again just one moment of being in the right place at the right time had a permanent effect on so many lives.

Another situation comes to mind in which my friend Ron had a house at a community called Pocono Country Place, and he invited a number of friends there for a winter getaway. So seven of us went one cold January weekend to eat, drink, play poker, and go skiing. We had a great time, and our wives were okay with us getting away for a boy's weekend. A few of us skied one day that weekend and it was my first time skiing at Camelback Mountain and we all had a lot of fun and a memorable day. So thanks to Ron owning that house and inviting us there, it resulted in me becoming familiar with Camelback, which resulted in returning there a year later to rent a house and go skiing with Barbara. This eventually led to us purchasing a home at the village at Camelback just a few steps from the ski slopes. Having this house enabled me to learn to ski much better and resulted in many family ski trips through the years.

But in addition, that weekend with the boys also had a profound effect on Ron's life because his next-door neighbor rented his home as a vacation home. That following summer, I made plans to rent that house with Barbara and my sons Eric and Tim. Our next-door neighbor Nancy, along with her son Tommy and her friend Arlene, also joined us. Ron had been divorced for two or three years, and I mentioned that he might want to go up to his house that same weekend since both of these girls were unmarried. We therefore invited Ron over to dinner one evening in which he met both women, and he had an immediate attraction to Arlene, as she did with him, and just a couple of years later, they were married. I guess one good turn deserved another, and Ron and Arlene had two children, and are still happily married.

I also often wonder how my brother Rob's life was impacted by watching how I lived my life. I was six years older, and I always studied and worked hard at school. He followed my lead after Saint Michael's and also went to Brooklyn Tech High School, but he was much more involved and became the school president. He then went to Columbia University in Manhattan, and upon graduation, he left home to attend law school at the University of Oregon. He wanted to go to law school in Boulder, Colorado, but divine providence led him to Eugene, Oregon instead. He met his future wife Brinda there, and they later moved to southern California. We visited them in California, and that encouraged my son Eric to also move to California at the age of nineteen, and he lived with them for a short while. In a couple of years, Eric met his wife Carla there and gave us two beautiful grandsons. Somehow, all of these events had a preordained reason.

So why am I telling these stories? I guess it is because they had such an impact on the lives of others, and it is amazing how paths chosen in life can affect so many various outcomes. And just perhaps they were also part of God's plan for my life.

Chapter 15

TAKING POSITIVE ACTIONS

In all of the circumstances that I mentioned in this book, there was one factor that was common to all of them and that was the fact that I acted quickly once a situation or an opportunity presented itself. I guess I can credit this ability to my DNA since it is totally unexplainable. Moments in life can disappear in an instant, and I recall that old saying, "seize the moment." So don't lose an opportunity that has been presented without taking action. That would be my advice to anyone reading this story.

In my case, taking action was something that I did automatically and without any reservations, and it is without a doubt one of my greatest assets. I acted immediately when I saw the posting outside of the dean's doorway, and I acted quickly when I first set eyes on Barbara and walked over to talk to her. The day I went to Con Edison, I came home and took action that led me to Rotork, and when I spoke to the gentleman at Killington, I wasted no time and quickly reached out to a real estate agent. Finally, when I went on Zillow and saw the house for Tim, I immediately drove by that house and miraculously met the owner.

So in that way, I took advantage of every one of these inexplicable circumstances that were put in my path, and I acted on all of them in a positive way. That was always the final piece to the puzzle, and the critical step that led to the final result. However, even though this was the case, I still know that I cannot take any of the credit for these situations or for taking these actions because they were all due to God's divine intervention in my life. There can be no other explanation. And so I can think of no other way of praying other than by giving thanks always for His putting me on my path and leading my way by His continual intercession and blessings. It's not something that I ever felt worthy of, and I know now that it was out of my control.

But somehow, He's guided me each and every day along the many paths that I've traveled in my life, and He also helped me to avoid all of the pitfalls that could have changed things drastically. Therefore, I felt that I was compelled to write this book at this point as I move closer to life's final journey. I am hoping that others will also be able to relate and find meaning and events in their own lives that will lead them to the same simple but amazing conclusion.

P hil Guarrasi is the son of a World War II vet and a native of Brooklyn, New York. He attended Saint Michael's Grammar School and graduated from the Polytechnic Institute of Brooklyn with a bachelor of science in aerospace engineering in 1970. He and his wife Barbara have been married for fifty years and have three sons and three grandchildren. Phil has also operated a business specializing in industrial valve automation for over thirty years. His other pursuits include a love for European travel and a passion for downhill skiing.